Contents

About the Author

The Secret Speed Cop has been involved in traffic law for thirty years and with Speed Cameras since the very beginning, even before Safety Camera partnerships were set up. Before the Government realised fines from speed camera offences could cover the running of the office, the staff wages, the equipment; all paid for by the motorist who drives too fast.

There when the Government decided education may be better than fining people and created speed awareness courses.

Many hours have been spent advising motorists about speed limits, explaining why they can't be 'let off'. stood in the witness box to tell Magistrates how the system works, how everything has been done legally and to answer any challenges that a driver or solicitor might wish to offer.

They were there when motorists kicked up a fuss about cameras being grey, sneaky and invisible, when it was decided they should all be painted bright yellow.

Did the bright yellow boxes slow drivers down? No. They still drove too fast.

Why?

Lots of excuses have been heard over the years.

Ignorance? I didn't know what the speed limit was: How did you pass your test then? If you didn't see the big, round signs with a number in the middle, should you be driving?

Disregard? The speed limit was too low so I took the law into my own hands, it applies to everybody else, not me.

I was late for an appointment/meeting/lunch with granny? Better to be late than not at all. Or, try leaving home earlier.

I sneezed and the reaction caused my foot to temporarily press down on the accelerator just at the exact point where the camera was: Yeah, right.

I was keeping up with traffic: If the rest of them drove off a cliff, would you follow too.

The driver behind was up my backside making me go faster. How was he making you? Was he pushing your accelerator down? Threatening you with a shotgun?

I was overtaking: If you need to speed to overtake then you don't need to overtake as the other car must be driving to the limit.

My speedo was broken. That's another offence to add to the list then.

Medical emergency. Probably the only one to cause some sympathy, sometimes. If it's a matter of life and death maybe. But, even then, if your mind is not concentrating on driving what could be an offensive weapon in the wrong hands should you really be driving at that time?

Drivers say speed cameras are a cash cow. A cash cow is a service that makes a steady income over a long period. So, maybe they are, except they don't 'make' lots of money, the money covers the cost of running the office so there is no profit.

And it's only because drivers keep allowing themselves to be caught by the cameras that the money is there to cover the cost of running the office.

If nobody speeds, there'll be no income so no money to pay for the office and, consequently, the office staff would be out of work.

Drivers say speed cameras are a tax on the motorist. No, they're not. You *have* to pay tax, you have no choice. But you do have a choice with a speed camera, you can choose not to speed.

You can see the Secret Speed Cop is experienced in his field and knows what they are talking about, why they obviously need to remain anonymous and why they are qualified to advise you on how you can avoid one of those speeding tickets dropping through your letter box.

By the end of this booklet, you should be in a position, yourself, to know how the system works and how you can avoid those pesky points on your licence.

Why do we have speed cameras?

Once upon a time, drivers could drive as fast as they liked without fear of being caught.

Well, not really, but that was how it seemed to the driver.

The only way they would be caught is if they passed a traffic cop with a speed gun and local drivers soon learned all their hiding places so could slow down when they got near. Nowadays, a speed trap by a traffic cop is a rarity. Now the driver is more likely to see a speed camera or one of the mobile camera vans. And whilst you know where your local fixed speed cameras are so you can slow down to 'get away with it', those mobile vans can pop up anywhere.

Unfortunately, with all that speeding, collisions occurred and people died.

Back in the 1940's over 7000 people were killed on Great Britain's roads every year, an astronomical amount considering how few vehicles there were on the roads. But then they were early days of driving, no tests, limited awareness of the danger, blackouts etc.

In 2001, about the time when Safety Camera Teams began to pop up around the country, there were 3450 people killed on the roads.

Nine years later, the number of deaths almost halved; in 2010 the figure was 1857; but, since then, the number has plateaued with 1870 road deaths in 2019. Although 2013 saw the lowest total of deaths since records began of 1713.

Obviously, not all of those deaths were due to speed. However, statistics show that over a quarter of all fatal accidents were caused by speed, whether that be excess or inappropriate. All the other fatals were caused by a variety of reasons, such as drivers not giving way at junctions or overtaking when it's not safe or inattention when driving so that shows the most common singular cause of somebody dying in an accident is speed.

Since speed cameras took off, the number of road deaths has halved. That's not all down to the speed cameras, of course.

Vehicles have better braking systems now. They offer better protection for the occupants, with roll bars and side protection bars. Some cars can even stop themselves, they have lane correctors to keep you on the right road and various other safety features all help to protect the road user.

But when you realise the amount of miles driven on British roads between 1993 and 2019 has increased by 50%, it can't leave much doubt that those yellow boxes on the side of the road are having an effect on causing the number of collisions to decrease.

Certainly, statistics show that collisions around the area of a fixed camera will decrease after installation.

As long as those cameras keep catching the speeding driver, they are going nowhere so the driver needs to know how not to be caught by them.

Why are they placed where they are?

The Safety Camera teams will normally place the fixed cameras in areas where there have been a high number of people killed or seriously injured. They will check to see if the collisions were as a result of high or inappropriate speed and do some Speed Data Recording to see if there is a speeding problem. If it all tallys up then a camera can go in.

If you want one in your area ask your local council but, if they say no, it's good in a way because that means not many people have been hurt.

The mobile vans can operate anywhere, usually as a result of complaints from locals. Again, they will do some speed data recording and, normally, if more than 10% are driving too fast, and there is a safe place to park and erect their tripod, then expect a van to visit.

Many residents then wish they hadn't complained about speeding along their road as we often find that the biggest offenders are the locals.

Contrary to popular belief, it is possible to operate the mobile cameras at night.

Types of Speed Camera

All cameras have to be approved by the Home Office. They are not allowed to be used until they are Home Office Type Approved so Safety Camera Offices will not buy a camera until it's HOTA, as they say in the trade.

They must also all be calibrated by the manufacturers, yearly usually but sometimes every two years, to make sure they are working correctly. A certificate will then be issued. The Safety Camera Team will not use one if it's not calibrated.

Some Camera Teams have a website where you can view the calibration certificate for the camera used. If not, you can write and ask to see it. You might be lucky and have a copy sent to you. But many Forces will say it's evidence which is only available if you contest it in court.

Some drivers query the calibration certificate when they see it as it generally says calibrated to 100 metres yet the driver has been caught more than 100 metres away.

However, that doesn't mean the camera is not accurate.

Each camera could be slightly different but, in the main, they can detect speeds at a distance measuring range of between 20 metres and 1,000 metres. The distance linearity is tested between 25 metres and 150 metres. When the system passes the tests on these restricted range of values, the system is certified to be calibrated throughout the full range of distances and speeds, therefore can measure at any distance between 20 metres and 1,000 metres.

Likewise, if the Force has a public access website, you will be able to view a copy of the photo that was taken. Or you can write and ask to see it. Again, they may send it. Some might not, citing the additional evidence line. Don't expect the photo to show the driver. They are intended as proof of the offence not to help you identify the driver. Some might help but many of them are taken from the rear so are no help at all.

Don't contest it in Court if you know you were speeding, take responsibility for your own actions.

And you were the driver so you know, in your heart of hearts, whether you were speeding or not. You might be angry at being caught, might feel a sense of injustice, that it's not fair but, at the end of the day, it's you driving so there is nobody to blame but yourself.

Being found guilty in Court will not only cost you a fine and points on your licence (as you would have got with the fixed penalty but probably higher), you will also have costs and a victim surcharge imposed. And the Court will find you guilty 9999 times out of 10000. The police wouldn't bother to let it go to court if they didn't think you were guilty.

Of course, if you have nine points on your licence or were driving at a high speed then you will have no choice about a court case, the police will automatically send you there.

Fixed

That bright yellow box at the side of the road. Also known as 'spot' speeds because they measure your speed at a certain point on the road.

I won't go into the minute detail of each individual sort because they all operate in a similar way.

In the beginning, these were mostly called Gatso's. Quite a big box on a pole, like the one many readers may remember *Max and Paddy* chopping down in the Peter Kay and Paddy McGuinness comedy series.

Illustration 1: An early Gatso

They originally used wet film which had to be collected by a camera operator and sent for developing. Of course, they are now digital so the images are transmitted, wirelessly, to the back office. This means they can be on all the time because the film won't run out.

Gatso Digital take pictures from the rear, so they can catch motorcycles. A radar works out in milliseconds how fast the vehicle is going and, if it's over the threshold, two pictures will be taken, half a second apart. The white lines painted on the road are a secondary check for the back office staff who, if need be, can use a time and distance check to confirm the speed travelled.

Similarly, Truvelo also make a digital spot speed. These measure the speed using two pairs of piezo-electric sensors embedded in the road surface.

Their signals are processed by two totally separate circuits within the instrument. Consequently, the two speeds are measured entirely independently from each other. If the speeds differ very slightly, then the instrument uses the lower of the two speeds, which is then rounded down to the benefit of the motorist. If the two measured speeds differ by more than 2 mph then the instrument gives a zero reading and no photograph will be taken. Therefore, a sensor based speed measurement system cannot produce an incorrect speed measurement.

Illustration 2: Truvelo Camera

All these cameras can monitor traffic heading in both directions.

It's no good trying to claim you have been blinded by the flash from the camera either. The Gatso will be from behind so might make you jump but is unlikely to blind you through your rear view mirror. For front photography operation, the flash must always be covered by a magenta coloured filter. The use of a magenta coloured filter gives rise to the popular misconception that infra-red illumination is used. It is not infra-red.

It's not law that they have to be yellow. However, motorists complained that the original, grey ones were not very visible, making them covert, a trap so the Government introduced guidance that they should be painted yellow. If you got caught by one that wasn't yellow, technically, the offence could still stand in a court.

The Highways Agency use a super high tech camera on motorways, called

HADECS, which are capable of monitoring five lanes of traffic at once. They use radar to record the speed of the vehicle.

So, to avoid being caught by a spot speed camera you simply need to slow down as you go past one, over the white dashes on the road.

Of course, if you jump on the brakes and slow down suddenly then you run the risk of being hit up the backside by the vehicle behind so, if you are driving over the thresholds (and you'll learn what they are later and why your speedo can also help you be slower than you thought) it's best to slow as soon as you see the camera or, better still, just drive at the speed limit. If you don't see the camera then perhaps you need to reassess your awareness whilst driving?

Average

In my opinion, these are the best for slowing traffic down over a longer area rather than just in one spot. However, rather than being about £25k to install, they are upwards of £250k!

The camera system is designed to accurately measure the average speed of vehicles over a measured distance. It uses pairs of video cameras that are installed at the roadside a measured distance apart. The cameras constantly monitor passing traffic. When a vehicle passes the entry camera, the system captures an image from the video and uses Automatic Number Plate Recognition (ANPR) software to read the licence number from the registration plate. It also records the time the vehicle passed the camera. When the same vehicle passes the exit camera, it again captures an image, reads the licence number and records the time.

The system can then pair the images of the vehicle together using the licence number. As it knows the exact distance between the entry and exit cameras, and the times that the vehicle passed them, it can calculate the vehicle's average speed. If the vehicle is exceeding the set speed threshold the offence details are kept. If the vehicle is not exceeding the threshold all the recorded information is discarded.

These cameras operate 24 hours a day, recording details of vehicles that exceed the speed limit threshold and automatically transmitting the offence data to the Safety Camera Office via a secure link for processing.

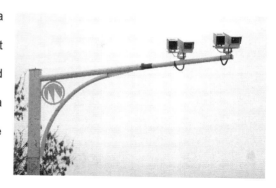

Illustration 3: An Average Camera

You have to laugh when you see drivers slowing down as they pass a yellow gantry with a camera on and then putting their foot down once they pass it until they get to the next one when they slow down again. You can drive past the gantry at 20mph if you like but, if you've driven between them at 100mph, it will take your picture.

The only way to fool this system, if you like to drive quick, would be to stop somewhere between the cameras for an hour or so, which probably defeats the whole reason why most people drive fast - to get somewhere quicker! Oh, and not all the cameras will be Live so you won't know if it's the first or second or even the fiftieth that was being used as the Entry cam and the second or fifty-first or whatever as the Exit.

The other way to avoid being caught is to make sure your speed doesn't drift over the threshold too many times for the entire length of the average camera system. If you go over by ten miles an hour for half a mile, drive the next half a mile at ten miles less than the speed limit. And hope the live cameras were not in that bit where you were ten miles an hour too fast.

More on thresholds later.

Mobile

Mobile cameras are what motorists commonly refer to as 'speed guns'; the ones you see operators, or occasionally police officers, using at the side of the road when they appear to be pointing a hair dryer at you.

Some of these 'guns' detect your speed by laser, others by radar. Basically, they are used to back up the operators belief that the vehicle is speeding (or not).

Illustration 4: A handheld speed camera

Laser handheld speed camera guns use a narrow beam of light about 10cm wide. This laser beam bounces from the target vehicle and provides the operator with a speed reading. The speed is displayed within 0.5 seconds of pulling the trigger. The gun carries out several diagnostic checks when it is switched on, if it fails any then it will not work.

Some of the guns have a range of 1km. If you have one of those laser speed detectors fitted in your car you can see it won't have long to warn you of the camera beam, by which time it will be too late to slow down. And, with a 1km range, they will have captured your speed long before you even see them.

Radar handheld devices use radio waves to target a vehicle. As a vehicle passes through the radio waves, these are reflected back at the radar receiver allowing the handheld radar gun to work out how fast the vehicle is travelling. The speed reading takes a couple of seconds and the range of these systems is about half a kilometre.

One thing to be aware of...these cameras are technically a secondary check to confirm the expert opinion of a Police or Camera Enforcement Officer that a vehicle is exceeding the speed limit and to obtain an accurate speed reading. The officer thinks you are speeding so pulls the trigger, he doesn't aim and shoot at every vehicle.

In theory, the court could believe his opinion you are speeding without any other evidence, the speed gun just confirms the officer's opinion.

As well as thinking that you only commit an offence if the camera is painted yellow, other drivers believe there has to be warning signs advising that cameras operate in the area. There doesn't.

They are put up though, to remind drivers, to give them a further opportunity to check their speed, to try and help them avoid the hassle of a speeding fine.

Yet still, despite all the warnings, 2.2 million drivers were caught speeding on UK roads in 2020.

That was 10% down on 2019 but, considering 2020 was full of lockdowns where traffic dropped by 80%, that is a lot of drivers who either blatantly disobeyed the law or were simply ignorant of the speed limits.

Hopefully, after reading this booklet, you will not become one of them in future.

How do you know the Speed Limits

So now you know a bit about the actual cameras, what about the speed limits?

Speed limits in the UK usually range from 20mph up to the National Speed Limit, which itself varies depending on whether you're on a single or a dual carriageway.

The type of vehicle you are driving, and even if you are towing, can also denote the maximum speed you are allowed to drive so it is not necessarily straight forward to know how fast you can legally travel.

For example, if you are driving your car on a single carriageway, national speed limit road, you can usually travel at 60mph. However, stick a caravan on the back and you can only drive at 50.

Hire a van to move house and you will have a different national speed limit to the car you drove to the hire companies premises. Normally, the hire company do not make you aware of the different limits. If you drive a large enough Goods Vehicle, you should be aware that there is even a different speed limit in Scotland to what there is in England or Wales.

Whether you agree with them or not, speed limits are there, and are there for the reasons explained elsewhere in this booklet, to keep everybody safe.

To help you understand and stick to these basic laws of the road, I've produced a table below to keep you on the right side of the limit, even if you're driving a vehicle that requires you to know a different set of limits to the norm.

How do you know what the limit of the road is? Well, speed limit signs would have been some of the first pieces of road furniture you needed to identify when you were taught to drive so you've not really got any excuse for not knowing them.

They are unique, with a white circle surrounded in red with black numbers within. These cover 20mph, 30mph, 40mph, 50mph and sometimes 60mph.

In addition, there's the National Speed Limit sign, which is a white circle with a black diagonal line through it. This means the national limit applies, which is 60mph on single carriageway roads, and 70mph on dual carriageways.

The speed limit on a motorway is 70, generally. However, be aware that there may be flashing signs on overhead gantries, adjusting the speed limit. These are called variable speed limits. But the flashing sign makes it very clear what the speed limit is so there's no excuse if you get caught.

What about built up areas? The technical name for roads in built up areas is a restricted road.

In these busy situations, it can sometimes be difficult to work out the speed limit. However, the general rule is, if there are buildings and street lights lining the road, then the speed limit is 30mph unless there are signs saying otherwise. Speed limit signs will be posted at the beginning of the limit then smaller repeater signs will be placed on lamp posts or individual posts at regular intervals within the zone.

Another thing to know is that the speed limit begins at the sign, not a hundred yards past it, so you need to slow down as you approach the speed limit sign so that, by the time you reach it, you are actually driving at the new limit.

There is nothing in law to stop the police catching you speeding one metre passed the sign although, in practice, they wouldn't normally operate that close.

Speed Limits

As promised, here is a table showing you the speed limit of each type for each type of vehicle on the various different roads.

Speed Limits (unless signs say otherwise)	Built-up areas mph (km/h)	Single carriageways mph (km/h)	Dual carriageways mph (km/h)	Motorways mph (km/h)
Cars, motorcycles, car-derived vans and dual-purpose vehicles	30 (48)	60 (96)	70 (112)	70 (112)
Cars, motorcycles, car-derived vans and dual-purpose vehicles when towing caravans or trailers	30 (48)	50 (80)	60 (96)	60 (96)
Motorhomes or motor caravans (not more than 3.05 tonnes maximum unladen weight)	30 (48)	60 (96)	70 (112)	70 (112)
Motorhomes or motor caravans (more than 3.05 tonnes maximum unladen weight)	30 (48)	50 (80)	60 (96)	70 (112)
Buses, coaches and minibuses (not more than 12 metres overall length)	30 (48)	50 (80)	60 (96)	70 (112)
Buses, coaches and minibuses (more than 12 metres overall length)	30 (48)	50 (80)	60 (96)	60 (96)

Speed Limits (unless signs say otherwise)	Built-up areas mph (km/h)	Single carriageways mph (km/h)	Dual carriageways mph (km/h)	Motorways mph (km/h)
Goods vehicles (not more than 7.5 tonnes maximum laden weight)	30 (48)	50 (80)	60 (96)	70 (112) 60 (96) if articulated or towing a trailer
Goods vehicles (more than 7.5 tonnes maximum laden weight) in England and Wales	30 (48)	50 (80)	60 (96)	60 (96)
Goods vehicles (more than 7.5 tonnes maximum laden weight) in Scotland	30 (48)	40 (64)	50 (80)	60 (96)

Goods Vehicle speed limits

One of the most common reasons for drivers being caught speeding is people who have hired a van for the day. Not being regular van drivers, the hirers don't realise they have lower speed limits and hire companies don't appear to warn anybody.

As you can see, though, from the previous table, vans (Goods Vehicles less than 7.5 tonnes) have lower speed limits: 50 in a 60; 60 in a 70.

Most vans:

- have a lower speed limit than cars

- must follow the speed limits for goods vehicles of the same weight

But there is an exception. Vehicles under 2 tonnes laden (loaded) weight may qualify as a 'car-derived van' or 'dual-purpose vehicle'. These vehicles have the same speed limits as cars.

Car-derived vans:

Looks like a van but is built on a car chassis as a derivative of a car (and is less than 2 tonnes laden). There's not many, most are likely to be like a Fiesta, Corsa or Clio but without the rear windows and back seats. How do you know if yours is a CDV? It will tell you under body type on the V5 Registration Document (Log Book).

Dual purpose vehicles:

Dual purpose vehicles are exactly as they sound – built with two purposes. Constructed or adapted for the carriage both of passengers and goods and with a maximum laden weight of two tonnes, and are either:

- constructed or adapted so that the driving power of the engine is, or can be selected to be, transmitted to all wheels of the vehicle

or

- permanently fitted with a rigid roof, at least one row of transverse passenger seats to the rear of the driver's seat and will have side and rear windows - there must also be a minimum ratio between the size of passenger and stowage areas

So stick a second row of seats and add more windows in your transit and it becomes dual purpose! But you must amend your log book with DVLA for it to count.

Motorhomes

Motorhomes less than 3 tonnes laden have the same speed limit as a car. Over three tonnes though and check the table for the limit.

Motor caravans are classed as goods vehicles if they:

- carry goods for exhibition and sale

- are used as a workshop

- are used for storage

so watch out for the different limits that apply (see the table).

The Process

So, what happens after your vehicle is caught speeding?

- After a vehicle is detected speeding by either a Fixed Camera or one of the Mobile Van operators, or by a police officer who was unable to stop the vehicle, a Notice of Intended Prosecution (NIP) must be sent by first class post or recorded delivery to the last known Registered Keeper and it must be sent so that, in the normal course of the postal service, it would be expected to arrive within 14 days of the alleged offence.

That doesn't mean it should arrive on your doormat within 14 days. If it was sent first class on the thirteenth day (which would be extremely unlikely in the usual course of events) it could reasonably be expected to be delivered the next day (unless weekends or bank holidays are involved) so, if you do receive a NIP on, for example, the 16th day, it doesn't necessarily mean it is invalid. The law says it will be considered as being served two business days after it was posted. For that reason, most Forces won't post one after day 10 or 11. It would then be for the defendant (you) to prove, to a court, that it didn't arrive in time. David Beckham managed it but do you have the money to spend on a legal team like his?

The Registered Keeper is the keeper as shown by the DVLA at Swansea. So, if yours was leased or a company vehicle, then it might not be you. The company have 28 days to respond so, by the time you get it, it could be over a month later.

There is an exception to the need to post one and that is if you are actually stopped by an officer who will issue a verbal NIP to you instead.

- The person to whom the NIP is addressed MUST respond to the NIP either by:

- If they were the driver, fully completing the appropriate section. By fully completed that means completing all the parts the Force require you to fill in. The law doesn't say you have to sign it but, if there is a dotted line which says Signature....... then the Force require it so, if you don't sign, then that is classed as not being fully completed and you could end up in court for not completing it!

- If somebody else was the driver then complete the appropriate section with the drivers details. Some Forces allow this to be done online.

- If the vehicle has been sold a response must still be made. If you don't have the name and address then you must provide all the details you do know.

- The NIP is a legal document so must NOT be passed on to somebody else.

- Failing to complete and return the NIP is an offence under Section 172 Road Traffic Act 1988.

- Once the nomination is received, the police will send out a new Notice to the nominated person and keep doing so until a driver admission is received. The second and subsequent Notices, although still referred to as NIPs, are technically purely a requirement to supply the name and address of the driver, or a Section 172 request.

- Once a driver admission is received:

  - The driver will, if eligible, automatically be sent an invitation to attend a Speed Awareness Course. They will also have an option to pay the fixed penalty or request a court hearing if they prefer.

- If not eligible for a course they will be sent a Conditional Offer of a Fixed Penalty. They also have the option to request a court hearing.

- If the speed was too fast for a course and a fixed penalty, the matter will be taken straight to court.

- If a driver fails to complete a course or pay the fixed penalty then the matter will proceed to Court instead. At Court, if found guilty, a Magistrate will decide on the amount of the fine and penalty points. Costs and Victim Surcharge will also be applied.

Enforcement thresholds

Anybody who says they were fined for doing 31 in a 30 is probably lying.

The National Police Chiefs Council (NPCC) set out recommended thresholds for speed enforcement. Their recommendation is for enforcement to begin at 10%+2 above the speed limit.

This means that in a 30mph limit the lowest speed you will be caught at is 35mph.

In a 40 it will be 46;

50 = 57;

60 = 68

70 = 79.

Of course, some police forces could choose to ignore the recommendation but not many do. The Met and Lancashire allow you to go 1mph faster (at time of writing).

Despite the recommended thresholds, it is possible that a police officer will pull you over for being 1mph over the speed limit as it is an offence, although you would have to be a bit unlucky to be fined for it.

A bit of advice...if you do get pulled over, don't be a twat. The bigger a knobhead you are towards the officer, the greater your chances of a fine. 'Yes sir, no sir, sorry sir' could lead to 'on your way son' whereas 'shouldn't you be out catching real criminals' or 'I pay your wages' is most likely to cost you money.

The reason the NPCC suggest a threshold of 10%+2 is to allow for any discrepancy with the speedometer of the vehicle.

A speedo must never show less than the actual speed, and must never show more than 110% of actual speed + 6.25mph.

So if your true speed is 40mph, your speedo could legally be reading up to 50.25mph but never less than 40mph. Or to put it another way, if your speedo is reading 50mph, you won't be doing more than 50mph but it's possible you might actually only be travelling at 40mph.

To ensure that they comply with the law and make sure that their speedometers are never showing less than the true speed under any foreseeable circumstances, car manufacturers will normally deliberately calibrate their speedos to read 'high' by a certain amount.

That's why those Smiley face signs that Councils like to put up, which flash your speed at you as you approach, never show the same speed as your speedometer.

You can't rely on the speed shown by your Sat Nav either. Sat Navs calculate the speed by using a time and distance calculation. On a long, straight road the Sat Nav is more accurate than the speedo but bendy roads can distort the reading. Steep hills can also affect the reading as can the quality of the signal up to the satellite.

Also, be aware that if you change the tyre or wheel size on your vehicle then that will affect the speedometer reading. The vehicle speedometer works out the speed by the revolutions per second of the vehicle wheels. Therefore, if the wheel circumference changes, the calculation will be wrong and give an incorrect speed. So if you change wheel sizes then get your speedo recalibrated.

Even a brand new tyre with deeper tread can alter the speed shown on the speedo as can a tyre worn down to its tread depth. It might only be millimetres but, with the wheel turning several times a second, that can lead to miles on the speedo.

The calibrated speed guns that Police use will show the real speed.

Motorbikes.

The police don't like to admit it but, if you are on a motorbike, and you are driving towards certain speed cameras, you will be able to get away with speeding. The front facing cameras obviously cannot read the number plate on a motorbike because it is on the rear of the bike, as this image from motorcycle news shows!

However, not all speed cameras are front facing so beware.

And, if you take the mickey and continually go through a camera, the police will sit and wait for you and pull you over, as they did in the case the image is from where a rider continually sped at stupid speeds in a 30 limit.

With a mobile operator, an operator can move his speed gun so he can track the bike as it goes past and record the registration that way.

Many vans the operators use also have a camera on each side of the van recording every direction so they can see the plate that way so, sorry motorcyclists, the net is closing in!

Avoidance Tactics

If you get caught speeding you might as well just own up to it and take responsibility for your own actions. Even if you didn't realise what the speed limit was, as a competent driver you should have done. Hopefully, you will after reading this booklet.

You can come up with all sorts of excuses but the response will be to tell it to the Court and that, as previously mentioned, will cost you more. The court tend to say you were driving too fast so tough, unless it was a matter of life or death or some other very good excuse!

You could try to avoid the camera being able to read your number. Fit a reflective number plate or cover it in cling film or vaseline, if not the whole plate then maybe a couple of the characters. Taking off a cover of the screws that hold the plate to your car could also make some of the characters look different.

But, the staff in the back office check every picture. They have the ability to enhance the photo manually, invert the colours or adjust contrast, to give a clearer image of the registration.

They can also do Registered Keeper checks using partial registration numbers so, if a couple of characters can't be read, the computer can still find the correct one.

Splattering mud all over the plate could do the trick but then it is an offence to drive with an obscured number plate so it leaves you open to being pulled over and fined for that instead. It also looks suspicious to a traffic cop who will pull you over and make all sorts of checks. Is it worth the hassle just to avoid the possibility you might drive too fast?

Even mud can be seen through by back office equipment anyway and, as said earlier, the staff only need to be able to read a couple of characters to be able to find the vehicle.

Enforcement

If you are daft enough to drive too fast and get caught doing so, what will happen to you?

For those who are only fractionally over the speed limit, some drivers may be eligible to attend a Speed Awareness Course rather than get a fine and points on their licence. To be eligible you must not have completed a course within the previous three years and the speed of the vehicle must fall into a certain criteria (see the table below). It costs money to do the course and, thanks to COVID, these are now either in a classroom or online, your choice.

It's the price of these courses that gets split between the course provider and the safety camera office to keep them running.

Drivers who were exceptionally fast will be sent straight to Court. If you were doing 30 mph over the speed limit you can expect to be banned. At court, you will be fined, have court costs and a victim surcharge against you and, of course, points on your licence.

In between the Course and the Court there is the fixed penalty. This has been set at £100 and three points for several years at the time of writing this so may well have been increased by the time you read this! The money from fixed penalties goes to the Treasury and they need to recoup some cash following the COVID crisis and upping the fixed penalty could be a way to do it.

Most Forces follow the National Police Chiefs Council (NPCC) guidelines regarding the enforcement of speeding vehicles. The table on the next page shows what those guidelines are:

Speed Limit Exceeded	Speed to be offered a course	Speed to be offered a Fixed Penalty	Speed to be sent straight to court
30	35 - 42	43 - 50	51 and over
40	46 - 53	54 - 65	66 and over
50	57 - 64	65 - 75	76 and over
60	68 - 75	76 - 85	86 and over
70	79 - 86	87 - 95	96 and over

Is a Course Worth It?

The course aim is to contribute towards safer communities by increasing drivers' intention to drive at an appropriate speed within the speed limit.

Courses can be taken anywhere in the country they don't have to be taken in the same area you were caught. They are held in the daytime, evenings and at weekends.

You could choose an old-fashioned classroom based interactive workshop delivered by a nationally accredited trainer which takes 4 hours to complete. There is no driving involved.

Or you can choose, for the same price, on online course which you can do from the comfort of your own living room and these only take a couple of hours.

Why Choose a Course?

• No fixed penalty or penalty points, in fact it is generally cheaper than the fixed penalty, it doesn't show on your driving record and you don't have to declare it to your insurance company because its not a conviction. Be aware though as some Insurance Companies ask if you have completed a course then bump your premiums. I would suggest changing Insurance Companies if they do that. After all, you ought to be a better driver after being educated on a course!

• No test so you can't fail it.

• Professional guidance and advice. All instructors are usually Advanced Driving Instructors.

• A chance to update your driving knowledge. You probably haven't read the Highway Code since you passed your test.

Wriggling

Many drivers believe they are legal experts and can wriggle out of it basically getting away with taking no personal responsibility for failing to comply with the law or driving safely and putting other people at risk by coming up with various excuses to get off speeding. Let's dissect some common ones.

The camera was too close to the beginning of the speed limit:

Unlikely. Camera operators usually make sure they are at least 100 metres away from the start of a limit. But, even if they weren't, the speed limit begins where the speed limit signs are so you should be slowing down as you approach the signs to ensure you are at the limit when you pass them.

The speed limit isn't correctly signed:

There only has to be one sign at the beginning of the speed limit. In all likelihood there will be a sign on both sides of the road but there only needs to be one. There will also be repeater (reminder) signs, unless its a 30 denoted by street lights, in which case the street lights are the repeater signs. If you didn't see these signs, should you be driving at all?

The street lights were off:

This is a weird one that came up on some petrol head sites. If you are caught during the day, of course the lights aren't on! 30 mph areas denoted by street lights do not suddenly become a free for all at night because the Council decide to save money and turn the lights off at midnight. The law says there should be a 'system of lighting', it doesn't say the lights have to be on. It doesn't even say you need to be able to see them! And they are not on during the day anyway, however, we all know, it is still a 30mph limit.

The flash made me jump, go quicker and nearly crash:

Interesting. It flashed because you were speeding so you were already speeding when it flashed, that is why it flashed. The flash did not make you speed, the speed made it flash!

The flash nearly blinded me:

No, it didn't. But, even if it did, it was you speeding that caused it to flash.

The camera wasn't calibrated:

Do you really think the police would waste their time catching motorists using a dodgy device? It would be very unlikely the police would go to all the trouble of setting up a speed trap using a non-calibrated camera. You can ask to see the certificate, if they do not have a website with it on. Some Forces will send a copy, others won't, saying its additional evidence only available in court. Of course, in the highly unlikely event that it is expired, you can reasonably expect the Force to notice and withdraw the case before court but do you want to take that risk unless you know for certain?

The NIP was received after 14 days:

It may well have been but when was it posted? Are you the registered keeper at the DVLA? Only the first NIP has to be posted so as to be expected to arrive within 14 days. A hired or leased vehicle, or a company car or one where the seller hasn't completed the log book correctly will not be registered to you so your NIP could arrive months later.

The operator was not a Police Officer:

Maybe not, but it was an operator employed and trained specifically for the role and authorised by the Chief Constable to detect speeders on his behalf.

There were no signs warning speed camera was in operation:

Actually, in law, there doesn't need to be. There is no legal requirement. Whether they are there or not, the speed limit is still in force. However, the police will place warning signs out along routes, out of the goodness of their hearts, as a nice reminder to drivers.

I don't know who the driver of my car was:

Really? Do you let any Tom, Dick or Harry out with your car keys? The owner has a legal responsibility to know who was driving their vehicle at any time. They should make sure that person has a Driving Licence – you know, are they actually competent to return your vehicle in one piece? The owner should check the driver is Insured to drive – you know, otherwise you're paying for everyone's damage. How about if the driver knocked over and killed a child, I bet you'd know who it was then. Not providing the drivers details is an offence in itself which carries more penalty points than the actual speeding offence. Falsely nominating somebody is also an offence for which you can be imprisoned.

I'm allowed to speed because I was overtaking:

The speed limit is the maximum. If you need to speed to overtake then you shouldn't be overtaking. There is no exemption in the speeding laws that says "oh, but it's alright if you want to get past the vehicle in front who is complying with the law." Technically, if you are doing just one mile an hour over the limit then you are breaking the law and could be reported

I was just keeping up with the flow of traffic:

Oh, that's alright then. If they were all driving off the top of the white cliffs of Dover, would you have kept following? You have your own accelerator and brake and speedo to use.

I sneezed/a bee;wasp;fly;ladybird was flying around the car:

At the exact same moment you passed the speed camera? Causing your foot to twitch down on the accelerator you say? Which made your car suddenly and immediately go quicker? Sounds legit!

Its not fair, why didn't you get the car in front of me:

How do you know we didn't?

My neighbour/brother/sisters aunties cousin is a speed freak who never gets caught.

They will.

What happens in Court?

If you really feel that a mistake has been made and you were not speeding or that you have good mitigation for breaking the law then you always have the option to take the matter to court.

You will also find yourself taken to court if you ignore any course offer or don't complete the fixed penalty.

Completing the fixed penalty means making the payment and sending off your licence to the HMCTS Fixed Penalty Office. Many people forget this bit and in this age when everything is online it is pointless (unlike your driving record!). All the HMCTS do is send it back but, until the Government get to grips with bringing the law up to date and into the 21st Century, then send it you must.

Some drivers have no choice about going to Court. If they were driving too fast to be offered a Course or Fixed Penalty or if they already have points on their licence and another three will take them up to or over 12 when they are then liable to be disqualified.

Once it is taken to Court, you only need to attend if you want to, which you should if you want to present your mitigation. Or if you plead Not Guilty. Or if you are liable for disqualification.

In the Courtroom, the Police Prosecutors, or sometimes CPS solicitors, will present their evidence. The defence can then counter to try and throw doubt on the matter or to offer the mitigation for speeding. Other witnesses will be called.

The Magistrate is neutral. They will listen to both sides of the story and make a decision based on the facts presented to them.

Be aware though, if it goes against you, not only will there be a fine, which will be a lot higher than the fixed penalty, there will also be the prosecution costs and there will be a Victim Surcharge on top as well. And you will still get the penalty points.

So, think very carefully before deciding to take the matter to court because, unless you have an absolutely watertight case, the police will have lots of evidence against you.

They might even call expert witnesses to explain, in minute detail, how the cameras work and won't be wrong. They even have experts who can calculate the speed just from analysing the two pictures and working out how quick you travelled between two pieces of roadside furniture.

And, if the Court find against you, you will be the one who has to pay the costs of the police witnesses which could run into thousands of pounds.

Laser Jammers

I'm sure many of you at some point would have considered buying a jammer.

A jammer is designed to block or scramble the laser signal back to the camera operator's speed gun.

They are often advertised/disguised as parking sensors or garage door openers. They are useless against the fixed cameras which detect speed by sensors in the road surface or the average cameras which measure time/distance.

Not to be confused with speed camera detectors, which simply tell you where the cameras are, a jammer is not illegal to buy or sell but it is illegal to use.

Don't think that the operator won't know if you are using one, they will. For a start, the speed of your vehicle won't show on their speed gun. And the guns will show an error message or code.

And, if they look close enough at the picture, they are quite likely to see it.

Whilst they might not have recorded the speed of your vehicle, they would have recorded your vehicle's registration plate.

That means you can expect a knock on your door from the police as they come to arrest you for perverting the course of justice, an offence which can carry a custodial sentence, which is happening more often.

In 2021, a 64 year old man was jailed for 8 months for having one fitted to his Mercedes. Just to avoid a £100 penalty and three points.

I wonder if he thinks it was worth the cost of the device now?

Wouldn't it be a travesty if you had a jammer fitted but were driving at 60 in a 60 limit, so doing nothing wrong, but the jammer caused an error message on a speed cops gun. You could end up in prison for attempting to pervert the course of justice when you were not even committing a speeding offence in the first place!

The Crux of the Matter

Now we get to the reason you paid for this booklet.

I dare say many of you came straight to this chapter!

How do you avoid a speeding ticket?

If you have read from the beginning then you have learned why we have laws to stop you speeding and why we have speed cameras.

You have read what the different types of camera are and how they work.

I have explained what the speed limits are, how you can tell what the speed limit is and told you that some vehicles have lower limits than cars, so be aware.

You've read about the enforcement thresholds – how far over the limit you could maybe get away with driving, and how your speedo will always show you are travelling faster than you actually are. Even how the tyres tread depth or size can effect the reading on the speedometer.

I've explained the process that happens should you get caught, what the police are legally required to do and what their enforcement options are.

I've told you some of the excuses people have tried, and usually failed, in order to 'get away with it'.

And you've been told what would happen to you in Court.

So, all in all, you now have all the information you need to avoid a speeding ticket.

You should now know what the speed limits are and how to work them out from signs and street lights and the type of vehicle you are driving.

You should now know that you can tell the speed you are travelling simply by looking at the vehicle speedometer which, as long as it is working correctly, should show you driving a couple of miles an hour faster than you actually are.

You should now be aware that the police have heard just about every excuse under the sun, none of which will make any difference to them and they will still enforce the offence anyway.

You, therefore, now have every tool you need to avoid a speeding ticket.

That's right, the cheapest, easiest way to avoid a speeding ticket is:

- know the speed limit

- look at your speedo to make sure it isn't reading a higher number than the said speed limit

- then, simply, keep that speedo at or below the speed limit.

In other words, to avoid a speeding ticket simply drive within the speed limit.